Five
Marks
of a
Methodist

"Steve Harper goes to the very heart of
faithfulness as he describes and then calls
upon all those who follow Wesley to live.
It is lives of integrity that are the result
of following these marks. Harper rightly
says this will give the ring of truth to our
daily living. He then goes on to identify
the 'Marks' or 'Practices' that when
followed will result in a life of
righteousness, goodness, peace, and joy.
It is a way of living in God's gracious
presence that he encourages for everyone,
and it is a way of living I choose
for myself."

—Rueben P. Job

Five
Marks
of a
Methodist

The Fruit of
a Living Faith

Steve Harper

Abingdon Press
Nashville

FIVE MARKS OF A METHODIST:
THE FRUIT OF A LIVING FAITH

Library of Congress Cataloging-in-Publication Data

Harper, Steve, 1947-
    Five marks of a Methodist : the fruit of a living faith / Steve Harper.
        pages cm.
    Includes bibliographical references.
    ISBN: 978-1-5018-0059-7 (binding; hard back : alk. paper)   1. Christian life—Methodist
authors.   I. Wesley, John, 1703-1791. Character of a Methodist.   II. Title.
    BV4501.3.H3567 2015
    248.4´876—dc23

                                                                                                    2014038735

Unless otherwise noted, all references to *The Works of John Wesley* are from the continuing Bicen-
tennial edition series published by Abingdon Press (1984–). Hereafter, all references to *The Works
of John Wesley* will be cited as Works with the corresponding volume and page number.

The Character of a Methodist is also available through this link: http://www.umc
mission.org/Find-Resources/John-Wesley-Sermons/The-Wesleys-and-Their-Times/The-Charac
ter-of-a-Methodist.

The quotations from Wesley come to us in the syntax of eighteenth-century English. To make these
five marks as accessible as possible, some pronouns in Wesley quotations will be substituted and
marked by italics where Wesley meant all Christians, male and female. Some pronouns, such as
"thee," will be rendered as "you" (except where poetic rhyming would be compromised).

17 18 19 20 21 22 23 24—10 9 8 7 6
MANUFACTURED IN THE UNITED STATES OF AMERICA

Marks

Character

Buildings last because they rest upon solid foundations. Without a good foundation, they may exist for a while, but they can't stand for a long period of time. Similarly, John Wesley understood that Methodism could begin and remain vital when it is built upon a good foundation. In his treatise entitled *The Character of a Methodist*, published in 1742, he describes the features of a good foundation.[1] He describes it in terms of "distinguishing marks"—the foundation that would establish a Methodist person or group on the right foot and sustain them for one lifetime after another.

Wesley didn't understand these marks in any isolated or sectarian sense, but rather as a life of discipleship lived in relation to the scriptural principles and practices that all Christians have followed since the time of Jesus. He had no interest in creating a separatist movement in the body of Christ, even though he was accused of doing so. As a wise spiritual guide, he knew that Methodism, like any movement, couldn't continue to exist if it was only the expression of a fleeting experience with God. No matter how genuine such an experience might be, other factors had to be in place if a person or group was to remain alive to God. So, in *The Character of a Methodist,* Wesley provided a solid foundation for the early Methodist movement in particular, and one that is necessary for any follower of Christ.

We live in a very experience-oriented time in history. We are rightly drawn to those people, places, and things that have what J. B. Phillips called "the ring of truth"—a mark of authenticity and relevance. In a world where words are cheap and character is counterfeited, we want to be assured we are giving ourselves to something real. When we see it, we are willing to invest in it, and we usually do so through some kind of deeply meaningful experience. But it doesn't take us long to discover something more is needed to sustain the original encounter. In fact, we usually learn that we can't sustain all the ways we felt at the beginning, because some experiences were not meant to last forever. Instead, we must move into a more intentional life that nourishes and expresses what first got us started.

John Wesley found himself in a similar place and time. Between about 1733 and 1738, he was overseeing a growing number of Christians who wanted to live their lives according to the gospel and do so in ways that held them accountable to each other.[2] By 1742, this collection of people became an identifiable movement within the larger Christian church. Anglicans, Quakers, Puritans, Presbyterians, Lutherans, Roman Catholics, and nondenominational Christians turned to him for spiritual guidance.

Some of this movement occurred outside of London and beyond Wesley's ability to oversee everything taking place. In anticipation of what would soon become the Annual Conference—the yearly gathering of leaders who prayed to discern what they were supposed to believe, teach, and do—Wesley wrote the foundational document called *The Character of a Methodist,* to provide the sustaining strength for what Methodism would become.

His original document remains a gift to us today. In it Wesley gives us five marks to confirm our identity as genuine and fruitful disciples and followers of Christ:

1. A Methodist Loves God
2. A Methodist Rejoices in God
3. A Methodist Gives Thanks
4. A Methodist Prays Constantly
5. A Methodist Loves Others

I offer this brief book to give you the opportunity to meditate on each of these characteristics and prayerfully apply them to your journey with Jesus. If you are part of the worldwide Methodist or Wesleyan family, you can come out of your reading with a greater knowledge and appreciation for why and how you follow Jesus. If you are located in another part of the body of Christ, you can emerge with a solid foundation to keep your spiritual house standing strong, a foundation made up of the five marks, which when taken together, John Wesley called *character*.

Steve Harper

1
A METHODIST
LOVES GOD

"What then is the mark?
Who is a Methodist, according to your own account?"
I answer: A Methodist is one who has "the love of God shed
abroad in the *heart by the Holy Ghost given* to us."*

—*The Character of a Methodist,* paragraph 5

A Methodist Loves God

"Teacher, what is the greatest commandment in the Law?"
He replied, "You must love the Lord your God with all your
heart, with all your being, and with all your mind. This is the
first and greatest commandment."

—Matthew 22:36-38

We live the Christian life in relation to the two great commandments: the command to love God, and the command to love others. Directly or indirectly, everything else emerges from this way of love. John Wesley knew this. He had steeped himself in the Christian tradition, which was itself rooted in love. So first he wrote that a disciple loves God.[1] By beginning with love, Wesley connects the rise of early Methodism with the essence of the gospel—with the very words of Jesus, and with the core motivation for everything that followed between the first and the eighteenth centuries. There was no other bona fide

way to begin any Christian movement, awakening, or re-
vival apart from the way of love. Wesley knew it; we must
know it too.

Our life in Christ begins in the fact that we love God.
We are like Peter, sitting with Jesus on the shore (John
21:15-19) and hearing him ask three times, "Do you love
me?" There is no other starting point for the life of faith or
the journey of discipleship. Jesus has to ask us more than
once, as he did Peter, because we are prone to wander away
from this core reality. And even if we find ourselves saying
that we do love God, the repeated question forces us to
look beneath the surface of our response to see what we
mean by it.

"Do you love me?" Jesus focuses our understanding
of love in relation to a world that alleges to love all sorts
of things. Some of our loves are illegitimate, and must be
challenged by Jesus. But even when we embrace genuine
loves, we must allow God to ask us if they flow from a
divine center, or if they are a random collection of deep
affections. The question "Do you love me?" isn't Jesus's way
of excluding other loves but rather his way of bringing all
our loves into a supernatural and holy relationship. And
as Jesus said in referring to the love of God as the first and
greatest commandment, it is a love that brings us (heart,
whole being, and mind) together into a unified person-
hood. As Parker Palmer puts it, we are divided no more.[2]

In many ways, love of God was John Wesley's keynote theme for the rest of his life and ministry. We see it continuing in his sermon "Scriptural Christianity" (1744) where he lays the foundation of the love of God in ways that are remarkably similar to what he said in *The Character of a Methodist*. While looking at the first Christians on the Day of Pentecost, Wesley noted, "This then was the very essence of his faith...the love of God the Father."[3] This is an interesting way to put it, because "the love of God the Father" can either mean God's love to us or our love to God. John Wesley wanted the early Methodists to read it both ways, first receiving God's love into our hearts by the Holy Spirit, and then responding to that love by enacting the two great commandments.

There is no greater day in the Christian life than when we discover that salvation means *wholeness*. It doesn't merely mean going to heaven when we die; it means living abundantly while we are here. But for this to happen, says Jesus—says Wesley—we must love God. Having received God's love first (1 John 4:19), we love God in return with everything we are and have. We do it in relation to every aspect of our life. We do it every day and to everyone. This is the first and foremost mark of a disciple.

But what kind of love is Jesus talking about? What kind of love does Wesley want the Methodists, indeed all Christians, to have? The Greeks had four words to describe it: *phileo*, *eros*, *storge*, and *agape*.[4] The Christian life includes and is committed to all four. But the word used to describe the essence and foundation of God's love is agape. Unlike the other three words, this quality of love is based in the lover, not in the one being loved. In fact, the other person may not be very lovable. The other person may not be wanting our love—or at least not appearing to do so. But with agape we love anyway.

This is exactly how God loves us, and many of us have experienced this kind of love. We have experienced what Charles Wesley called "amazing love" and what John Newton called "amazing grace."[5] This is what Paul meant when he wrote, "But God shows his love for us, because while we were still sinners Christ died for us" (Rom 5:8). In the past we may have laughed at the thought of God, run from the presence of God, or spit in the face of God, but what we received in return was God's love—variously described in the Bible as faithful love, loyalty, mercy, patience, forgiveness, and redemption, to name a few qualities. We now realize that if God's love had been anything other than agape, none of us would be here. The whole foundation would have crumbled long before now.

But . . . we are here. We are alive. We aren't destroyed by sin; we are saved by grace. Light overcomes darkness. We are unable to run from God without also running into God. This is what John Wesley and others call prevenient grace, the love that moves the hymn writer to pen, "O, Love that will not let me go; I rest my weary soul in thee!"

We are dearly loved by God![6] And nothing can separate us from that love (Rom 8:35-39). Only the word *agape* describes this—the most radical kind of love possible. Unconditional. Unrelenting. Unending. Unbelievable!

The first mark of discipleship isn't a call to increase our love but to receive God's love. The ability to love God comes from God! This is no self-help effort, no intensification of our devotion through a spiritual version of trying harder. The call to love God is a call extended by none other than God. The desire to respond with love is a desire put into us by God. As Eugene Peterson put it,

> First God. God is the subject of life. God is foundational for living. If we don't have a sense of the primacy of God, we will never get it right, get life right, get *our* lives right. Not God at the margins; not God as an option; not God on the weekends. God at the center and circumference. God first and last; God, God, God.[7]

A great danger in much of contemporary spirituality, Christian and otherwise, is that it keeps the focus on the self—the ego.[8] And the peculiar thing about egotism is that it will let us believe in God and claim to love God, but always on our terms—no matter how sophisticated or subtle the affirmations may be. The sign of egoic faith is that we orient our love in terms of personal benefit, even our love of God. "Have it your way" becomes more than a hamburger-chain slogan; it becomes our life's motto. But the kind of love the gospel describes, and the kind of love Wesley affirms, is radically different.

It doesn't take very long for us to realize that this isn't a natural love; it is supernatural. Left to ourselves, we will love those whom we think are lovely. We will love others as long as they love us in return. We will love others for what we can get out of it—whether short-term or long-term. Wesley's call to love is one to which we respond, "I can't do this on my own!" This is right where he wanted the people called Methodist to be: people who renounce all attempts to love from the source of self, and who now receive the invitation to love from the source of grace. We manifest our love through phileo, eros, and storge, but the simple source of faithful love is agape—the love of God that first possesses us, and then enables us to love that way in return.

God is the first object of our agape love, because if God isn't our first love, we end up loving God for reasons that the self seeks. We will love God for what we can get out of the relationship. We will love superficially and capriciously. Instead, we must love as one who has "the love of God shed abroad in his heart by the Holy Ghost."[9]

By naming the first mark of a disciple to be a person who loves God, Wesley is inviting us to step into the stream of scripture and tradition; to join with the first followers and the subsequent saints who have made the love of God their heart's desire, a desire made possible because we are made in the image of God; that is, created with the desire

8

and the capacity to receive and give life. Our incentive to do this is born out of God's first love of us. By making the love of God the first mark, Wesley is leading us to embrace the disposition of our hearts, from which everything else flows. And as he points out, it is a love that makes God the joy of our heart. Let the power of Wesley's words sink into us:

> *God is the joy of our heart, and the desire of our*
> *soul,*
> *   which is constantly crying out,*
> *"Whom have I in heaven but you?*
> *   and there is none upon the earth that I desire but*
> *   you!"*
> *My God, and my all!*
> *   You are the strength of my heart,*
> *   and my portion for ever!*[10]

Here are words we could ponder every day for the rest of our life. We need to read them over and over, allowing them to descend deeper and deeper into us. We yearn to be saturated with these words. They open the door to our whole being, commencing a journey that moves us from superficiality to substance, start to finish. We move beyond churchianity (good as it is) to Christianity. We move from membership (good as it is) to discipleship. Many of the people to whom Wesley ministered were already members of a congregation. To them, he exhorted a deeper life in

Christ, one that included, but transcended, institutional identification.[11] To those who were outside the church, he called them to become members of a Christian community somewhere, but to see it as a means to the greater end of loving God regardless of institutional affiliation.

As we can see from Wesley's exclamation above, the love of God produces joy. The church is necessary and good, but it isn't perfect. If we stop with the love of church, we will eventually be disappointed and hurt. A profession of faith is necessary and good, but it isn't the sum total for the Christian life. New birth is essential, but it only makes us spiritual infants. New birth is where we begin, not end, our discipleship. If we stop with a doctrinal faith, we will eventually be discouraged as we see fellow believers hotly debating it, and ourselves coldly living it. So there is only one place to begin: the love of God. Here is the source, the supply, and the life—of every disciple. The love of God is the goal to which we aspire, and it is the means by which we reach it. A disciple loves God. Charles Wesley set this sentiment to music when he wrote,

> *Love divine, all loves excelling,*
> *Joy of heaven, to earth come down,*
> *Fix in us thy humble dwelling,*
> *All thy faithful mercies crown!*
> *Jesus, thou art all compassion,*
> *Pure, unbounded love thou art;*

Visit us with thy salvation!
 Enter every trembling heart.[12]

Markers

1. In your spiritual formation, which of the two commandments is currently calling for greater attention? Why?

2. How have you found the love of God to be the orienting center for your discipleship?

3. Consider how new birth is where discipleship begins, not ends. How have you found this to be so?

2

A METHODIST
REJOICES IN GOD

"Rejoices evermore!"

—*The Character of a Methodist,* paragraph 6

A Methodist
Rejoices in God

Don't be sad, because the joy from the LORD is your strength.

—Nehemiah 8:10

When one of my best friends sends me a personal note or e-mail, he ends the correspondence by using these words: "with His joy." For him, the phrase is much more than a happy-go-lucky way of ending a communication. It captures the spirit of biblical living. My friend has lived long and deeply in God. He and his family have experienced the ups and downs of life, the successes and failures, the joys and sorrows. But on any given day, if I receive a message from this mentor, it will likely end with the words "with His joy."

While standing in the stream of the Christian saints, John Wesley included joy in the first mark of discipleship when he said, "God is the joy of his heart." But rather than let it go at that, he made rejoicing in God the second mark of discipleship. He shows us that joy (like everything else) flows from the love of God, but rather than being blended into love in some kind of amorphous way, joy stands on its own as a distinctive evidence that we are living as Jesus's disciples. With an echo of Nehemiah's words to the people, Wesley was saying, "The joy from the LORD is your strength."

As a teenager in the 1960s, during the civil rights movement, I was too young to leave home and join those who were singing, marching, suffering, and dying for freedom. I read everything I could find by Martin Luther King Jr. including *Strength to Love*.[1] Martin knew what every saint has learned: it takes *strength* to love, and the primary expression of strength is joy. This is one reason why the civil rights movement included both sermons and singing. It is why the early Methodist movement included John the preacher and Charles the hymn writer. *The Character of a Methodist* is a treatise that begins and continues like a sermon, but ends with a song. Before Jesus and his disciples left the upper room and headed for Gethsemane, they sang a hymn (Matt 26:30).

What role does joy play in following Christ? Simply this: discipleship is a whole-life response to grace. We make a mistake when we define the spiritual life only in terms of its religious dimensions. We fail to grasp what God is offering us when we limit it to the cognitive element. Joy is the word used by Christians in every age to describe the comprehensive response we make out of our whole being to God's love. That's why Wesley made joy the second mark of a disciple. And from that simple word *joy*, he moved on to further define it.

He begins with happiness. He says that a disciple is "happy in God." Wesley was trained in classical thought, which understood happiness in terms of the Greek concept of *eudaemonism*. Don't let the strangeness of the word throw you. It is the reason why Wesley was quick to name joy as a mark of discipleship. Far from being a fleeting or superficial emotion that only occurs when we are getting our way, classical "happiness" is a deeply ethical word that means the harvest of a life given over to righteousness. The bond of being loved by God and loving God in return produces a quality of life that can only be found in a relationship with God. But when it is, happiness is the life of virtue and goodness that emerges. For Wesley, happiness of this sort was so powerful and transformative he used the word to begin each of the Beatitudes in his translation of the New Testament. For him, it was the hallmark of the more-often used word *blessed*. The Common English Bible also translates the Beatitudes with the term: "Happy are people who have pure hearts, because they will see God....Be full of joy and be glad, because you have a great reward in heaven" (Matt 5:8, 12).

When we have this happiness, we have peace—peace based on the fact that perfect love (the union of God's love for us with our love for God) casts out fear (1 John 4:18). Joy is a mark of discipleship that gives us confidence and courage. This is an essential ingredient because as long as we evaluate our Christian life in terms of what others think of us, we will play it safe, which is to live in fear. Perfect love is the genesis of courage—courage rooted in love— courage that fills us with joy. It is different from a bull-in- a-china-shop spirituality, which claims to be courageously prophetic when it is actually only obnoxious. Instead of this, we live in joyful peace knowing that when we are faithful to God we are living not only as God intends but doing so in the right spirit.

E. Stanley Jones made this kind of happiness one of the hallmarks of his message. By using words remarkably similar to Wesley, he wrote, "It is no mere accident that joy follows [from] love. Joy is a by-product of love."[2] He tells of passing by a place in Los Angeles that had this sign on the outside: Jones Jolly Joint. He wrote, "I laughed and said, 'That's me on the inside.'"[3] Wesley would have liked that way of putting it, for the joy he has in mind for disciples comes from deep within—from the indwelling of the Holy Spirit, who produces the fruit of the Spirit in and through us, beginning with love, and then joy—joy with peace and patience.

The basis for our joy, Wesley writes, is the atonement, the moment and the process where we are reconciled with God. Jesus's death upon the cross is the objective proof of God's love (Rom 5:8), and because he died for us, we can live for him. We do this because we know our sins are forgiven. Wesley observed that the disciple rejoices over deliverance from "the horrible pit" with "all his transgression blotted out as a cloud." Here is the basis for our assurance, and here is the motivation for our readiness to forgive others.

This is why we pray through the Lord's Prayer, "Forgive us the ways we have wronged you, just as we forgive those who have wronged us" (Matt 6:12). The little word *as* takes us in more than one direction. It means in ways that are comparable. So we pray, "Help us forgive others in ways similar to God's forgiveness of us." It can also mean simultaneity. So we pray, "In the midst of experiencing God's forgiveness, give us the desire to forgive others." We are God's forgiven and forgiving people! This reconciliation with God and with others is the source of our joy.

This assurance becomes the incentive for our hope. Wesley says that our redemption not only provides present blessings, it also gives us a vision of "the glory that is about to be revealed" (1 Pet 5:1). Again, drawing on ideas given by Peter, Wesley calls this a *living* hope. It is an experience of God that isn't deferred but rather one that is real in the present moment. Anticipation doesn't produce postponement. And all of this, Wesley writes, is for *me*—not in the sense of selfishness but in the sense of being applied uniquely to each and every one of us. Like fingerprints that make us unique and unrepeatable sons and daughters of God, we are given a distinctive soul print—not just the life of God in the human soul but the life of God in *my* soul. Wesley had a conversation with the Moravian minister August Spangenburg upon arrival as a missionary in Georgia. Spangenburg asked Wesley if he knew Jesus was his savior. Wesley replied, "I know he is the savior of the world." But Spangenburg wouldn't let it end there. He asked again, "But is he your savior?" Wesley responded in the affirmative, but later wrote in his journal, "I fear they were vain words."[4] The Spirit of God began to move in Wesley's heart, showing him that God isn't interested in a vague, impersonal relationship but is interested in a heart-to-heart, life-to-life relationship that connects to the unique people that we are. On this basis, we can move into each day of our lives "with God's joy." A disciple rejoices in God. Charles Wesley took this conviction and set it to music:

> *Rejoice the Lord is King!*
> *Your Lord and King adore;*
> *mortals, give thanks and sing,*
> *and triumph ever more.*
> *Lift up your heart, lift up your voice;*
> *rejoice; again I say, rejoice.*[5]

Markers

1. Reflect on the phrase "discipleship is a whole-life response to grace." What two or three thoughts come to your mind?
2. Respond to the statement, "Joy is the mark of discipleship that gives us courage and confidence."
3. Why do you believe that reconciliation with God is crucial in giving our joy its proper meaning?

3

A METHODIST
GIVES THANKS

And you *who* have *God's hope...* "in everything give thanks."

—*The Character of a Methodist,* paragraph 7

A Methodist Gives Thanks

Thank God for his gift that words can't describe!

—2 Corinthians 9:15

Wesley's third mark is that disciples, or Methodists, give thanks. While we might think of these marks as "simple," we don't mean that they are easy. In fact, some expressions of the marks are impossible to do on our own. None of the marks are achievable apart from grace. We note this now because Wesley uses Paul's words to describe the third mark: "Give thanks in every situation because this is God's will for you in Christ Jesus" (1 Thess 5:18). I have been a Christian for more than fifty years, but every time I read these words I still think, "Whoa! We have gone to the deep end of the pool with this idea."

It isn't that giving thanks is something we resist. But Paul said we are to do it "in every situation." Wesley said the same thing in the treatise, and he strengthened the point by writing, "From him therefore he cheerfully receives all, saying, 'Good is the will of the Lord.'" At a depth of faith that is sometimes inaccessible to me, I believe these words are true. But on any given day, I question the mark—sometimes profoundly.[1] How are we to give thanks "in every situation" when some situations seem to come not from the will of God but from the pit of hell? There is no way to sidestep this reaction in the life of discipleship, because it happens to all of us sooner or later, directly or indirectly. We have good reason to begin this chapter asking Wesley, "John, what are you saying?"

Unfortunately, John doesn't provide a fully satisfying response. But of course, no one ever has or can. We know that Wesley was not a pie-in-the-sky or Pollyanna-ish person (as his words and notations in his journal clearly show). He was not a naïve Christian, and he was not the least bit interested in launching a sentimental movement. So we read and apply *The Character of a Methodist* in general, or this third mark in particular, in the context of realism. The third mark is shaped by several key elements.

First, Wesley rightly notes that *gratitude* is the Christian's response to God. Gratitude is the response to grace. Anne Lamott gets it right in her book *Help, Thanks, and Wow,* when she shows how saying "thanks" is always our first response when we recognize that God has helped us.[2] Her conviction is similar to Paul's exhortation and Wesley's

26

third mark of discipleship. Wesley practiced this character-
istic each Saturday in his own prayer life.[3] After praying the
previous six days in relation to the two great commandments (love God and love others) and the spirit of surren-
der that attends them, Wesley came to Saturday recogniz-
ing that his life had been lived in relation to God's grace in
both large and small ways. He used each Saturday to look
back upon the week just lived, to note God's providences,
and to express his gratitude for them. He expressed it in
these (updated) words:

> God, *you* the great creator and sovereign Lord of heaven
> and earth, *you* the father of angels and *human beings*,
> you the giver of life and protector of all *your* creatures,
> mercifully accept this my morning sacrifice of praise
> and thanksgiving, which I desire to offer, with all hu-
> mility, to your divine majesty.[4]

He continued by recounting what we might call the
most general blessings he had received, and then moving
into more specific acts of God's goodness toward him. Each
Saturday evening, he continued the same theme of gratitude in his prayers, but also by asking himself particular
questions for self-examination in relation to thankfulness:

1. Have I allotted some time for thanking God for
   the blessings of the past week?
2. Have I, in order to be the more sensible of them,

seriously and deliberately considered the several
circumstances that attended them?

3. Have I considered each of them as an obligation
   to greater love, and consequently, to stricter holiness?[5]

When we stop to remember that Wesley prayed this
cycle week after week for more than sixty years, we can see
how the words of prayer would eventually become a life of
prayer, with each week of his life climaxing with a response
of gratitude.

Second, when we take John Wesley's entire life and
ministry into account, we find that gratitude is grounded
in the nature of God, not in the circumstances that were
taking place in his life at any given time. Without trying to solve the problem of evil or justify the reasons for
suffering, Wesley did seek to establish the foundation for
goodness—the nature of God, who is Love. He would
agree with Jesus's parable of the weeds and the wheat, that
the weeds are sown into the world by "an enemy," not by
God (Matt 13:28). He would disavow the insurance company claim that hurricanes, floods, and other disasters are
"acts of God." Instead, he would see every form of evil
as a violation of God's will. Neither germs nor grenades
reveal the world God intends. We may never know why
things happen as they do, but we do know that God isn't
the author of evil. We may find ourselves caught in the

net of mystery when it comes to understanding the days of our lives, but we can always know that God isn't taking any delight in the bad things that happen to us or to anyone else.

Unless we spend time on this spiritual practice of gratitude, we will never find the third mark of discipleship within us. Charles L. Allen was for many years senior pastor at First United Methodist Church in Houston, Texas. In his generation of ministry, he was arguably the best-known Methodist pastor in the world. I had an opportunity to ask Dr. Allen some questions when he was one of the principal speakers for the annual ministry conference at the campus where I taught. "What is the number one problem you have had to deal with over the years of your ministry?" Without a moment's hesitation, he replied, "The number one problem I have had to deal with is the mistaken notion so many people have that God is mad at them." He observed that as long as people see themselves in the presence of an angry God, God can never become a meaningful part of their lives.

John Wesley would agree, and that is why he founded his theology and his ministry in love. As long as we think that God is mad at the world, and more specifically mad at us, we will hold God at arm's length. Like Adam and Eve, we will go into hiding when God comes near. But instead of this, we remember that God sought them out, called them to come out of hiding, and provided garments to cover the shame of their sin. That is what God does. That is what love does, and it is the basis for thanksgiving.

The way of love is the basis for Wesley's observation that a disciple "cheerfully receives all." We can only do that when we realize that no matter what happens to us, we aren't alone. We can only do that when we recognize that God is at work to deliver us from evil, which is exactly what we say every time we pray the Lord's Prayer. It is also what Wesley himself later experienced when he faced death. In the earlier part of life, his greatest fear had been the fear of death. But when he came to the hour of death, his last words were, "The best of all is, God is with us!" He died giving thanks.

So we as disciples give thanks—not for what is happening to us but for the fact that nothing can happen to us apart from the presence of God with us. This is what Paul meant when he said that "nothing can separate us from God's love in Christ Jesus" (Rom 8:38). We don't receive all people and circumstances because everything is good; we receive because God is present in everything, ready and willing to come to our assistance. Giving thanks is the reason why Wesley could say, using Paul's words again, that a disciple has "learned how to be content in any circumstance" (Phil 4:11). This is thanksgiving that combines faith with realism.

Wesley further develops the third mark of a disciple by showing that thanksgiving is a means of leading us out of anxiety. Because God is good, we can cast all our anxieties on God (cf. 1 Pet 5:7). We don't have to carry the weight of the anxiety itself or the burden of trying to figure out why something is happening to us. God cares. God knows. God gives grace. We live in the strength that these affirmations give. Thanksgiving is the evidence that we are staying in love with God.

Before moving on to the next mark of discipleship, Wesley connects thanksgiving to the ways we pray as disciples. In short, we can pray about anything and everything, because we know we are taking our petitions to the One who loves us! It is a great day when we live into the reality that we are never interrupting God. We are never a bother to God. This only increases our thanksgiving. We realize with joy that no matter how small or large, no matter whether it is day or night, no matter whether we understand what is happening or not, we can always "take it to the Lord in prayer." God's "open door" policy is the source of great thanksgiving.

When we step back from the particulars of this mark as Wesley describes it, we see that thanksgiving is the comprehensive response we make to life. It is the 24/7 understanding of the hymn writer's words, "Though the wrong seems oft so strong, God is the ruler yet."[6] We can describe this philosophically and generally, but most of us experience it in concrete ways. We know people who lead off conversations with negative attitudes or feelings.

We know people who approach life more as a problem to be confronted than a glory to be lived. If they do it time and again, we no longer look forward to being around them.

But then there are folks who wake up each day eager to live another day, doing so in the belief that God is good, present, active, and sufficient. They aren't naïve optimists; in fact, some of them live with personal debilitations, economic hardships, and family stresses that go beyond anything we are facing. But we look forward to seeing them or hearing from them because we know they will be living *into* life, not away from it. This third mark of the disciple is more than positive thinking or having a pleasant disposition—both of which are commendable. Rather Wesley commends the deep response to grace that produces the outlook on life that brings us to each day, and to the end of life itself, grateful for having had the privilege of living on this earth. A disciple gives thanks. Charles Wesley expressed this attitude by writing,

> *Incarnate Deity, let all the ransomed race*
> *render in thanks their lives to thee*
> *for thy redeeming grace.*
> *The grace to sinners showed*
> *ye heavenly choirs proclaim,*
> *and cry, "Salvation to our God,*
> *salvation to the Lamb!"[7]*

Markers

1. Where have you found it challenging to give thanks? Did any of the key elements in this chapter help you with that struggle?

2. What is your dominant concept of God? How has it helped shape your discipleship?

3. Where do thanksgiving and prayer currently intersect in your life?

4

A Methodist Prays Constantly

For indeed one *"prays without ceasing."*

—*The Character of a Methodist,* paragraph 8

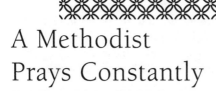

A Methodist
Prays Constantly

First of all, then, I ask that... prayers... be made for all people.

—1 Timothy 2:1

Discipleship is first and foremost a relationship between Jesus and us. It is a living reality described in John 15 as the connection that exists between a vine and a branch. We follow, learn from, and serve Christ as his dearly loved brothers and sisters. To make this clear, Jesus told the apostles, "I don't call you servants any longer, because servants don't know what their master is doing. Instead, I call you friends, because everything I heard from my Father I have made known to you" (John 15:15).

John Wesley described this shift in terms of his own experience, referring to it as the movement from being a servant to being a son.[1] He didn't mean that servanthood is abandoned but rather that it is put into a new context.

The entirety of discipleship moves from regulation to relationship, from the impersonal to the personal. Obedience is no longer marked by keeping the faith but by following Jesus—by remaining in him as a vine remains in a branch. This isn't a diminishment of faith, only a transplanting of it into new soil.

Every relationship is established and maintained by communion and communication, so it comes as no surprise that Wesley describes the Christian life in relation to prayer, making it his fourth mark of discipleship. Prayer is the way we create and sustain our relationship with God. John Wesley viewed prayer as a means of grace, saying that "the chief of these means is prayer, whether in secret or with the great congregation."[2] His view reflects the revelation of scripture and the witness of the Christian tradition, a view that draws from the words of Jesus himself in John 15, where he said that he heard from the Father and passed on what he heard. How did Jesus hear from the Father? Surely it was in his own times of prayer. How does Jesus make known to us what he has heard? Surely it is in those times we spend in prayer with him.

There is no fixed order to the marks, but it makes sense to put prayer after the love of God, our rejoicing in God, and our thanksgiving to God. If nothing else, putting it here reminds us that prayer is a response to God. This is mystery, but the fact is whenever we pray, we are in some way responding to a prior movement of the Spirit in us. We often say, "I need to pray more," but the truth is, we need to respond better. God is constantly speaking and showing; we are the ones who move in and out of consciousness with respect to God. The heart of a disciple is a heart of attentiveness, and devoting ourselves to prayer is the main way we confirm our desire to hear from God and then put what we have heard into action.

As a priest in the Church of England, John Wesley did this within the infrastructure of *The Book of Common Prayer.* Far from being a sterile ritual, it is filled with words that we *pray*, not just say. And as we do this, day after day over the course of our lives, the written prayers become living prayers. A look at *The Book of Common Prayer* quickly reveals that the prayers in it arise from the Bible itself, guide us into prayers we wouldn't think of on our own, and enable us to pray formally and informally with both structure and spontaneity. They give us an order for daily prayer,[3] weekly prayer, and prayer that follows the salvation story of the Christian year. From childhood, John Wesley's spiritual formation was shaped by this kind of praying. And as we have already seen, he made use of liturgical prayers when others asked him to teach them how to pray.

You may or may not be drawn to liturgical prayer as your preferred way of praying, but we must all be taught to pray in ways that keep us rooted in scripture, ways that open us to ideas and intercessions that aren't limited to our own experiences, ways that establish a pattern while still permitting our own needs to find expression. This kind of praying, whatever the style, can help us deal with wandering thoughts, and it can sustain us with true prayers when we go through times of spiritual dryness.

When John Wesley wrote *The Character of a Methodist,* these formative dynamics were likely in his mind, because he had been praying this way for decades. Even in his description of a disciple, "It is given *one* always to pray and not faint," Wesley would naturally see ceaseless prayer (with or without the accompanying feelings) as a manner of praying provided through liturgical prayer. But it is clear that formal prayers were only the infrastructural underpinnings for a larger life of prayer that expressed other kinds of praying. John Wesley prayed with words and in silence. He prayed alone and with others. He prayed when he felt like it and when he felt as if his prayers were making no difference. He prayed with the inspiration and guidance of the Bible and with the instruction of tradition. He prayed with the full range of emotions.[4]

Clearly, liturgical prayer isn't all Wesley has in mind when it comes to prayer. For he went on to write about prayer in a way that isn't bound to fixed formats and formal times:

> Not that *one* is always in the house of prayer—though *one* neglects no opportunity of being there. Neither is *one* always on *one's* knees, although *one* often is, or on *one's* face, before the Lord *our* God. Nor yet is *one*

always crying aloud to God, or calling upon him in words. For many times "the Spirit *makes* intercession for *us*, with groans that cannot be uttered." But at all times the language of *the* heart is this: "*You*, brightness of the eternal glory, unto *you* is my mouth."[5]

This kind of praying combines formality and spontaneity, fixed times and all time, times we are conscious of God and times when the Spirit prays for us. That is why Wesley summarized prayer in these words: "This is true prayer, lifting up the heart to God. This is the essence of prayer, and this alone."[6]

Here Wesley is drawing upon the scriptural imagery of focusing our heart on the Lord (e.g., Josh 24:23). We put all our attention on God, so that we can allow Jesus to do exactly what he said he wanted to do in John 15. The imagery of focusing, or "inclining" our hearts (KJV) gives us a picture of prayer as a spiritual "law of gravity." With our hearts directed upward, whatever God wants to send our way will roll directly into our minds and hearts. The primary disposition for this is listening, giving attention by faith that God will send into our lives whatever instructions and inspirations God wants to us have. The key element in prayer isn't what we say to God but rather what God says to us.

We should take great joy and comfort from this understanding of prayer. Over the decades of teaching prayer, people have often said to me, "I don't know what to pray for," or "I don't know what words to use," or "I get stage fright at the thought of praying out loud, so I avoid prayer groups." All these obstacles are overcome when prayer is a disposition of our heart. And because we are made in the image of God, with both the capacity and the desire to relate to God, that disposition is already present. It is what the apostles were expressing when they said, "Lord, teach us to pray" (Luke 11:1). The challenge of learning to pray is to connect with this disposition and move with it.

In one church, we began a men's prayer group. Larry told me he would come, but only if I would never call on him to pray, or expect him to pray out loud at any time during the meeting. I assured him that I would honor his request, and that I was happy to know he wanted to be present, even in silence. I had learned that one way to help people learn to pray in a group is to have prayer books on the table, books people could use to find a prayer they would be willing to pray during the prayer time.

At first, Larry didn't even do that. He sat in silence—a silence that I now recognize as more sacred than I did at the time. But then, one morning, as we were praying, Larry spoke aloud one of the prayers in a book. He found one that expressed his intentions, and read it to the rest of us with as much devotion as any of us had done in our spontaneous praying—perhaps even more. Once the ice was broken, he almost always did the same in future meetings. In fact, his use of the books on the table sparked conversation in the group about liturgical prayer that might not have occurred if he had not begun praying this way.

And then, one morning, as we were praying, Larry offered his own words in a simple prayer of thanks for the day. When he later shared with me his journey of prayer in the group, he said he discovered (in the atmosphere of safety and acceptance) that praying was not as complicated as he previously thought it to be. And there came a time when, after hearing other men pray week after week, he said to himself, "I can do that." On that occasion the desire of his heart connected to his tongue, and Larry prayed on his own.

This isn't a requirement for any disciple. In fact, in the Gospels, we never actually overhear a disciple praying. But we know they prayed. Perhaps one reason we don't have their prayers (even though we do have some of Paul's) is that God wanted to preserve the essential freedom given to us in the call to pray. There is no one-size-fits-all style. Silent prayer is as holy as spoken prayer. Praying a prayer from a prayer book is as sacred as praying in an unknown tongue. That's because prayer is the disposition of our heart toward God. Prayer is that holy ground conviction—"I can do that!"—made on the foundation of our heart's desire to be in communion with God.

As Wesley goes on to show, this understanding of prayer not only makes it possible for us all, it makes it possible anywhere, anytime:

In this *one* is never hindered, much less interrupted, by any person or thing. In retirement or company, in leisure, business, or conversation, *one's* heart is ever with the Lord. Whether *one* lies down or rises up, "God is in all our thoughts"; *one* "walks with God" continually, having the loving eye of *the* mind still fixed upon him, and everywhere "seeing him that is invisible."[7]

Wesley knew that by praying from the heart, it is possible to be fully engaged in the affairs of life while simultaneously being attentive to God. In this understanding of prayer, he stands in the line of those who, like Brother Lawrence, practiced the presence of God in the midst of daily routines.

We discover in the fourth mark of a disciple that Wesley has given us a vision and pattern for prayer that is for anyone, anytime, anywhere. It is impossible to remain stuck in an "I don't know how to pray" frame of mind. Like the first apostles, we can turn with hope to the praying Christ (the one who hears from the Father and shares what he hears with us), and ask him to teach us to pray, knowing that this is something he longs to do. We have no greater opportunity and privilege than to enroll in Christ's school of prayer, and move at his bidding into the life of prayer.[8]

Through liturgical and nonliturgical means, through fixed and spontaneous expressions, through corporate and personal times, God teaches us to pray. And as we continue in our journey of prayer, we experience the increase of joy because, "for this I was made!" A disciple prays constantly. Charles Wesley commended this by writing,

> *Pray, without ceasing pray*
>   *(Your Captain gives the word),*
> *His summons cheerfully obey,*
>   *And call upon the Lord;*
> *To God your every want*
>   *In instant prayer display;*
> *Pray always; pray and never faint;*
>   *Pray, without ceasing pray.*[9]

Markers

1. How does the idea of prayer as a response to God affect the way you pray?

2. Have you made use of liturgical prayer? If so, how have you found it to be helpful in your prayer life?

3. What does "pray without ceasing" mean to you, and how do you attempt to put the admonition into practice?

5

A Methodist
Loves Others

"One *who loves God, loves* our brothers and sisters *also.*"

—*The Character of a Methodist,* paragraph 9

A Methodist
Loves Others

The person who doesn't love a brother or sister who can be seen can't love God, who can't be seen.

—1 John 4:20

The fifth mark of a disciple is that we love others. Consumerism creeps into our spirituality like it does into almost everything else today. Left to ourselves, we can easily turn discipleship into a religious version of "What's in it for me?" When we read *The Character of a Methodist,* we immediately realize self-indulgence is nothing new. It was a concern Wesley had at the beginning of the early Methodist movement. It is a problem we have contended with since the Garden of Eden, as Adam and Eve succumbed to egotism and tried to be their own gods. This originating sin winds its way through the corridors of time, reaching us in this very moment. Consequently, the longest section of

Wesley's treatise is an exposition of the second great commandment: God's call to love our neighbors as ourselves (Mark 12:33).

Everything Wesley described in the first four marks is intended to be a spring of living water that can nourish those around us, as we love them in Jesus's name. We love God, rejoice in God, give thanks to God, and pray to God as a means of forming a personal communion with God that grows into the commission to live for God. Three of the most important words in spiritual formation are "in order that." We read the Bible in order that_____. We pray in order that_____. We worship in order that_____. We serve in order that_____.

This perspective doesn't bypass or minimize the personal benefits we are meant to have in our relationship with God, but it does keep us aware of the fact that we receive in order to give.

The second commandment becomes the conduit for God's love to flow through us after it has flowed into us. It is a love, Wesley says, "full of love to all *humankind*, to every child of the Father of the spirits of all flesh." And lest we think he was only thinking of fellow Christians, Wesley hastens to say it extends to people we don't know, and to people whose lives we don't approve of. It extends even to our enemies. In other words, it is the kind of love (*agape*) that isn't given because of the nature of the receiver but because of the nature of the giver. We explored this earlier in the first mark, and Wesley brings it up again, so we don't miss it. There is no more radical love than this—to love everyone—regardless. And this is the kind of love God commands and the kind of love Wesley commends.

As with the first commandment, to love God with our whole heart, mind, and being, we are brought back to the necessity of grace if we are to love in this way. Apart from grace, we will love other people conditionally, and worse still, we will set the conditions for giving our love! When this happens, our discipleship becomes ego-driven rather than Spirit directed. The call to love others is a call to love radically—to love from what Wesley describes as a pure heart. This is a heart purified from

> all revengeful passions, from envy, malice, and wrath, from every unkind temper or malign affection. It cleanses *you* from pride and *a haughty spirit,* whereof alone *comes* contention. And *a disciple* has now "put on bowels of mercies, kindness, humbleness of mind, meekness, long-suffering," so that *one* "forebears and forgives and forgives, if he had a quarrel against any; even as God in Christ hath forgiven *you.*" (Col 3:13 KJV)[1]

All such behavior is rooted in our intention, what we desire to do. Here Wesley is drawing water from the wells of early Christianity. For example, in John Cassian's first *Conference,* he uses the image of the archer, reminding us

that we can't expect to hit a target we aren't first aiming to
hit. Of course, other things precede and follow the aim,
but where there is no aim, there is no archery.[2] Similarly,
our discipleship becomes what we intend for it to be. That's
why the Christian life is given its fundamental shape by
the two love commandments, the first and the last mark
of Christian character: "You must love the Lord your God
with all your heart, with all your being, and with all your
mind . . . and love your neighbor as yourself" (Matt 22:37-
39). We have identified the target. And as Wesley shows in
this section of the treatise, it is this purity of intention that
enables all the rest to follow. He describes it this way:

> *Your* one intention at all times and in all things is, not
> to please *yourself,* but him whom *your* soul loves. *You
> have* a single eye. And because "*your* eye is single, *your*
> whole body is full of light" (Luke 11:34 KJV). Indeed,
> where the loving eye of the soul is continually fixed
> upon God, there can be no darkness at all, but "the
> whole light; as when the bright shining of a candle"
> (Luke 11:36 KJV) *does* enlighten the house.

To carry the idea forward, Wesley changes the meta-
phor from light to fruit. Rooted in the love of God, we
now bear the fruit of that love. The evidence that we are
doing this is that we keep God's commandments—"Not
only some, or most of them, but all, from the least to the
greatest." This isn't legalism. Rather it is obedience that

flows from the realization that every command of God is life-giving. Every command of God comes with the grace to carry it out. Every command of God comes with the presence of the Holy Spirit to assist us in fulfilling it. We do all of this, Wesley says, because our obedience is in proportion to our love—"the source from whence it flows."

At this point, we come to "vocational discipleship." The word *vocation* is a word too often bypassed in the formation of faith and discipleship. But it is the biblical word that describes why we do what we do in the first place, and defines the means by which we do it. We are called; that is, God speaks to us, and we live in response to what we have heard. That's the essence of obedience—responding to what we have heard. Good listening is the prerequisite to good living. Our discipleship isn't shaped and expressed through an impulsive selection of something good from a collection of random opportunities. It is shaped in response to the ancient prayer of Samuel: "Speak, LORD. Your servant is listening" (1 Sam 3:9).

Without this kind of prayerful listening, we can wander off the discipleship path by either beginning to make it up as we go along, or by becoming overwhelmed with too many good things to possibly do. If we wander off in the first way, discipleship becomes just another feel-good, self-help effort. If we wander off in the second way, discipleship becomes a minimalism fueled by the sense of futility. God has another way in mind for us—the way of listening that is followed by selected and specific activity.

Frank Laubach's morning prayer is an example of the kind of obedience Wesley wants disciples to have. He prayed, "Lord, what are you doing in the world today that I can help you with?"[3] The twofold wisdom of his prayer guided him into faithful living. First, the prayer reminded him that God is at work in the world. God doesn't wait for us to act, but rather invites us to join in on what is already going on. And second, the prayer reminded him there are some things God is doing that we aren't expected to do. Laubach recognized a kind of spiritual distribution plan, where each disciple is given her or his assignment— a measurable and achievable amount of the will of God. E. Stanley Jones had a similar perspective when he wrote about going each morning to his "listening post" to get his marching orders for the day.

This assignment—this portion of gospel living—is most often attached to the work we do every day. The saints of the ages refer to this as "ordinary holiness." It is further symbolized in the longest portion of the Christian year that we call "ordinary time." We see it in Jesus's first call to the apostles, when he told them he would teach them to fish for people (Mark 1:17). He was talking to fishermen! This was his way of saying, "Take what you normally do and naturally do, and do it for me." Suddenly, discipleship isn't a course to take and pass, but rather it is an offering of the life we live routinely. Eugene Peterson captures this idea in his paraphrase of Romans 12:1 in *The Message:* "So, here's what I want you to do, God helping you: Take your every-day, ordinary life—your sleeping, eating, going-to-work, and walking-around life—and place it before God as an offering."

This kind of discipleship dawned upon Kiefer during the evening meeting of a couples group. I proposed that we name the apostles. This was not too difficult, and in relatively short order we had the twelve named. Then I said again, "Name the apostles." Quickly the list was expanded to include the likes of Paul and Junia. A third time I beck-oned them to "name the apostles." At this point, the ex-pressions on the faces of everyone changed, but they gave it their best shot, adding names like Euodia and Synteche to the list.

When I called for a fourth round of naming, there was awkward silence. Kiefer broke it after a few moments by asking me, "What are you asking for, preacher? Do you want us to put our names on the list?" In that moment, by the grace of God, Kiefer added his name to the list! If he were with you as you read these words, he would tell you that was the moment his discipleship came alive in a new way—the moment he put his name on the list, and began living for Jesus where he was and as he was.

Until we realize that we are called to live in day-sized compartments, and to do so in and through the regular

activities of our lives, discipleship will easily appear so for-
midable that we will be tempted to settle for membership
in the institutional church rather than an all-in investment
in God's kingdom. But when we realize that God's desire is
to use us as God has made us, everything changes. We still
need grace to live this way, but now it is our real life made
holy and offered to God.

Henri Nouwen described this kind of discipleship as
living "here and now." Failure to do this, he said, turns
the spiritual life into a fantasy life—a life where we can
imagine being spiritual somewhere else, or at some other
time, but here, not now. Instead, we must recognize
and receive the sacredness of the present moment and the
current location. In order to do this, he wrote, "we must
believe deeply that what is most important is the here and
the now."[4] Nouwen's words capture what Jean Pierre de
Caussade taught through his phrase "the sacrament of the
present moment." Wesley saw an example of this Christian
character lived out in his own mother's conviction (drawn
from Puritan heritage) that "every moment is a God moment."

The motive of everything Wesley presents is that "all
may come unto the measure of the stature of the fullness of
Christ." Discipleship connects us to others. We can't keep
from sharing God's good gifts to us. These include the tan-
gible possessions we have, and also the intangible qualities
that have made us who we are in Christ. So it is no surprise

that the fifth mark of a disciple is nothing other than giving what we have received.[5] It is no surprise that Wesley exhorts us to do this through the lives we live each and every day. This is the means by which we fulfill the second commandment. A disciple loves others. Charles Wesley enjoins such ordinary love in these words:

> *Summoned my labor to renew,*
> *And glad to act my part,*
> *Lord, in thy name my work I do,*
> *And with a single heart.*[6]

Markers

1. How do the words "in order that" move your inward experience of God into outward expressions of your faith?

2. What insights did John Cassian's analogy of the archer give to you?

3. Where do your discipleship and your vocation currently intersect?

On Your Marks

Wesley almost never ended his writings or sermons without some kind of practical application. His conclusion to *The Character of a Methodist* is no different. The final paragraph shows us what he wanted the early Methodists to do with all he had written. He drew upon the concept of practical divinity, which meant that theory must become practice—a profession of faith must become an expression of faith. Today we call it "lived theology."

In the last paragraph of the treatise, he writes of it with respect to the spirit and attitude that should characterize disciples who embrace and enact these five marks. Simply put, we are not to think of our discipleship in any way that separates us from any other Christian. These are not strictly or exclusively the marks of a Methodist; they are the qualities of life that any follower of Christ should exhibit. And when we do so, they should not only have a transforming effect upon us; they should draw us into relationship with all other believers.

So he wrote, "If any *person* says, 'Why, these are only the common, fundamental principles of Christianity—*So you say.*' So I mean." He quickly strengthens his view by adding, "I and all who follow my judgment do vehemently refuse to be distinguished from other *people* by any but the common principles of Christianity." Wesley's refusal to allow Methodism to evolve from a movement to a denomination in his lifetime was, in part, related to his belief that God had raised up the people called Methodist to be yeast in the dough of Christianity regardless of its institutional manifestation.

We dare not miss this point as we bring our look at the marks of a disciple to a close. Wesley's conclusion leaves us with two important truths. First, we are invited by God to develop our discipleship broadly, not just deeply. Our identification with a particular part of the body of Christ is normal, but at some point in our spiritual formation, we will feel the tug of the Holy Spirit to mature our faith from other traditions than the one we have chosen. At some point in our discipleship journey, we will be invited to drink from other wells.

Unfortunately, some misinterpret this universal tendency in practicing faith to dilute our character as Christians. However, openness to other traditions strengthens our faith. It recognizes what the writer of Hebrews wanted the people of the day to know, that we are *surrounded* by a great cloud of witnesses (12:1). To be surrounded means that we can look in all directions in the church and find a saint there to encourage us, guide us, counsel us, protect us, and support us. The cloud imagery is a reminder that these men and women come to us across the sky (spectrum and history), giving us a 360-degree discipleship. Every time and tradition holds something of value for us.

The second truth of Wesley's conclusion is that we are called to lower the walls of our particular identities just enough, not to eliminate valid differences but to be sure those differences don't become barriers in our love for each other. The world of Wesley's day and of our day does not know, or care, about the major and minor points that have given rise to thousands of denominations and parachurch organizations. In fact, our nit-picking and arguing confuses and turns off those who believe the church should be and do better. Our witness is diminished by our debating.

Neither must we allow differences to divide one Christian from another. We live in a time when Christianity is increasingly marginalized and caricatured by the world; we dare not do the same to each other. Robert Fulghum's call to "Hold hands and stick together" is a call to us.[1] It is the call to stand upon the foundation where there is "one Lord, one faith, one baptism, and one God and Father of all, who is over all, through all, and in all" (Eph 4:5-6). This kind of *oneness* is at the heart of the gospel, and it must be the leading edge of our life together and of our mission in the world.

When we lose this sense of unity, we begin to define ourselves by adjectives instead of nouns (e.g. Methodist Christian), but Wesley wants us to see that no matter who we are, or where we are, we are all part of nothing more nor less than "plain, old Christianity."[2] Here is the essence of our discipleship, remaining firmly in Christ, which makes us followers of Jesus "not in name only, but in *heart* and in *life*," a life in Christ in which we are "inwardly and outwardly conformed to the will of God as revealed in the written Word." In Wesley's view, a disciple is one who "thinks, speaks, and lives according to the method laid down in the revelation of Jesus Christ. A Christian's whole being is renewed after the image of God, in righteousness and in all true holiness. And 'having the mind that was in Christ' *one* so walks as Christ also walked."

The Wesleyan way of discipleship is a way for us all. It can be rooted in any particular soil, but it bears fruit that can't be limited to one particular field. The Wesleyan way of discipleship is a way of following Jesus into kingdom living, the very way that Jesus announced at the beginning of his ministry (Matt 4:17) and unfolded until the day he ascended into heaven (Acts 1:1-8). To the extent that we receive and embrace the five marks of a disciple found in *The Character of a Methodist,* we will be living a life not only that John Wesley would commend but one with which our Lord would be pleased. A disciple is a Christian. Charles

Wesley put this conviction into words in the final stanza of the hymn that John put at the end of his treatise:

> *Pour out your souls to God,*
>   *And bow them with your knees,*
> *And spread your hearts and hands abroad,*
>   *And pray for Zion's peace;*
> *Your guides and brethren bear*
>   *Forever on your mind;*
> *Extend the arms of mighty prayer*
>   *Ingrasping all mankind.*[3]

Notes

Character

1. *The Works of John Wesley* 9:67–75.

2. He wrote *The Nature, Design, and General Rules of the United Societies* in 1738 to help structure these early groups. Rueben P. Job provides a clear introduction to this foundational document in his book *Three Simple Rules* (Nashville: Abingdon Press, 2007).

1. A Methodist Loves God

1. Notice that Wesley's fifth and final mark in *The Character of a Methodist* is the second commandment to love others. In a very real sense, the two love commandments are the beginning and end of the five marks, just as they are the beginning and end of the Christian life.

2. Parker Palmer, *A Hidden Wholeness: The Journey Toward an Undivided Life* (San Francisco: Jossey-Bass, 2004), 9.

3. *Works* 1:161.

4. It is beyond the purpose of this book to go into detail about these Greek words. You can easily go online and find more about them.

5. Respectively in Charles Wesley's hymn "And Can It Be, That I Should Gain?" (363) and John Newton's "Amazing Grace" (378) in *The United Methodist Hymnal* (Nashville: The United Methodist Publishing House, 1989).

6. Trace this remarkable idea through the Hebrew word *hesed* and through the Greek word *charis,* also through the writings of Henri Nouwen, particularly his book *Life of the Beloved* (New York: Crossroad, 1992). Similarly, most of Brennan Manning's books draw us into God's amazing love.

7. Eugene Peterson, *Conversations: The Message With Its Translator* (Colorado Springs: NavPress, 2007), now called the *Message Study Bible*.

8. Here I would recommend the writing of Richard Rohr, particularly his books *Everything Belongs* (New York: Crossroad, 1999), *Falling Upward* (San Francisco: Jossey-Bass, 2011), and *Immortal Diamond* (San Francisco: Jossey-Bass, 2013).

9. In classic Christianity one of the most descriptive treatises on this subject is Bernard of Clairvaux's *Four Loves.* It is available in a wide variety of formats.

10. *Works* 9:35.

11. This is no basis for what is sometimes called today "churchless Christianity." A look at the larger life and ministry of John Wesley reveals his recognition of the holiness of the church and its necessary place in God's kingdom; the church is where persons are formed into Christlikeness. At the same time, he knew that to make the church an end rather than a means was to

misunderstand the body of Christ and the nature of the Christian life.

12. Charles Wesley, "Love Divine, All Loves Excelling," in *Works* 7:545.

2. A Methodist Rejoices in God

1. Martin Luther King Jr., *Strength to Love* (New York: Harper and Row, 1963).

2. E. Stanley Jones, *Growing Spiritually* (Nashville: Abingdon Press, 1978), 134.

3. Ibid.

4. This is a summary of a longer conversation. See *Works* 18:145–46.

5. Charles Wesley, "Rejoice the Lord Is King!" in *The United Methodist Hymnal,* 716.

3. A Methodist Gives Thanks

1. I write of this in more detail in my book *Talking in the Dark: Praying When Life Doesn't Make Sense* (Nashville: Upper Room Books, 2007).

2. Anne Lamott, *Help, Thanks, and Wow* (New York: Riverhead Books, 2012). The "wow" that comes third is a movement from the momentary expression of appreciation to an abiding sense of gratitude expressed as awe and wonder.

3. John Wesley, "A Collection of Forms of Prayer for Every Day in the Week," in *The Works of John Wesley,* ed. Thomas Jackson (Salem, OH: Schmul Publishers, 1979), 11:232. Wesley originally published the "Collection" in 1733 as a way to help his students at Lincoln College (Oxford University) learn to pray, expanding the publication later to include a wider audience who wished to do the same.

4. Ibid., 232–33.

5. Ibid., 235.

6. Maltbie D. Babcock, "This Is My Father's World," in *The United Methodist Hymnal,* 144.

7. Charles Wesley, "Maker, in Whom We Live," in *The United Methodist Hymnal,* 88.

4. A Methodist Prays Constantly

1. John Wesley, "On Faith," in *Works* 3:497–98.

2. John Wesley, "The Means of Grace," in *Works* 1:381.

3. Section 5 of *The United Methodist Book of Worship* (pp. 568–80) also contains orders for Daily Praise and Prayer.

4. I say more about Wesley's prayer life in my book *Devotional Life in the Wesleyan Tradition: A Workbook* (Nashville: Upper Room Books), 41–60.

5. *Works* 9:37.

6. Ibid.

7. Ibid.

8. In Luke 11, a first-grade approach allows Christ to give us the Lord's Prayer, as he did the first apostles—a liturgical prayer

that we can pray word by word, but also a pattern for prayer that makes the words windows into personal spontaneity.

9. Charles Wesley, "The Whole Armour of God," in *Works* 7:401. Note that this is the hymn that Wesley attached at the end of *The Character of a Methodist,* showing that the kind of "character" he has described in the treatise equips us to live the life of discipleship.

5. A Methodist Loves Others

1. *Works* 9:38, par. 10.

2. John Cassian, *Conferences* (New York: Paulist, 1985), 37–59.

3. J. Ellsworth Kalas, *The Will of God in an Unwilling World* (Louisville: Westminster John Knox, 2011), 61.

4. Henri Nouwen, *Here and Now* (New York: Crossroad, 1994), 19.

5. Wesley didn't leave the giving of love vague or up for grabs. A year after he published *The Character of a Methodist* (1742), he published *General Rules of the United Societies.* In this key document, Wesley gave what we today call the Prudential Means of Grace: do no harm, do good, and attend the ordinances of God. Thanks to the book *Three Simple Rules* by Rueben Job, we have an excellent way to study those means and incorporate them into our lives. It is a good thing to keep *The Character of a Methodist* and *General Rules of The United Societies* together as we develop our discipleship.

6. Charles Wesley, "For Believers Working," in *Works* 7:466.

On Your Marks

1. Robert Fulghum, *All I Really Need to Know I Learned in Kindergarten* (New York: Ivy Books, 1989), 5.

2. This isn't a passing phrase, but one carefully crafted by Wesley to describe historic orthodoxy; that is, faith that is at work in all, understandable to all, and applicable for all. It is a faith that avoids complexity on the one hand and superficiality on the other.

3. *Works* 9:45.